HEY-HO, TO MARS WE'LL GO!

A SPACE-AGE VERSION OF "THE FARMER IN THE DELL"

SUSAN LENDROTH

Illustrated by BOB KOLAR

iˆi Charlesbridge

The Rocket's on the Pad,

The rocket's on the pad,
Hey-ho, to Mars we'll go—
The rocket's on the pad.

When you jump up, gravity pulls you back down. Launching a rocket into space is hard because Earth's gravity is pulling the rocket in the opposite direction. The bigger and heavier the rocket, the more power you need to break free.

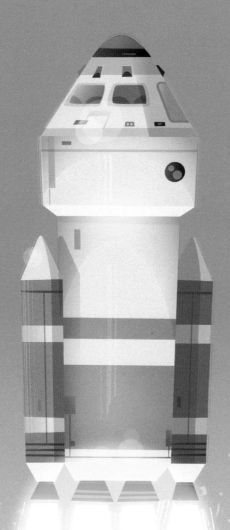

We launch with a roar,
We launch with a roar,
Hey-ho, to Mars we'll go —
We launch with a ROOOOOAR!

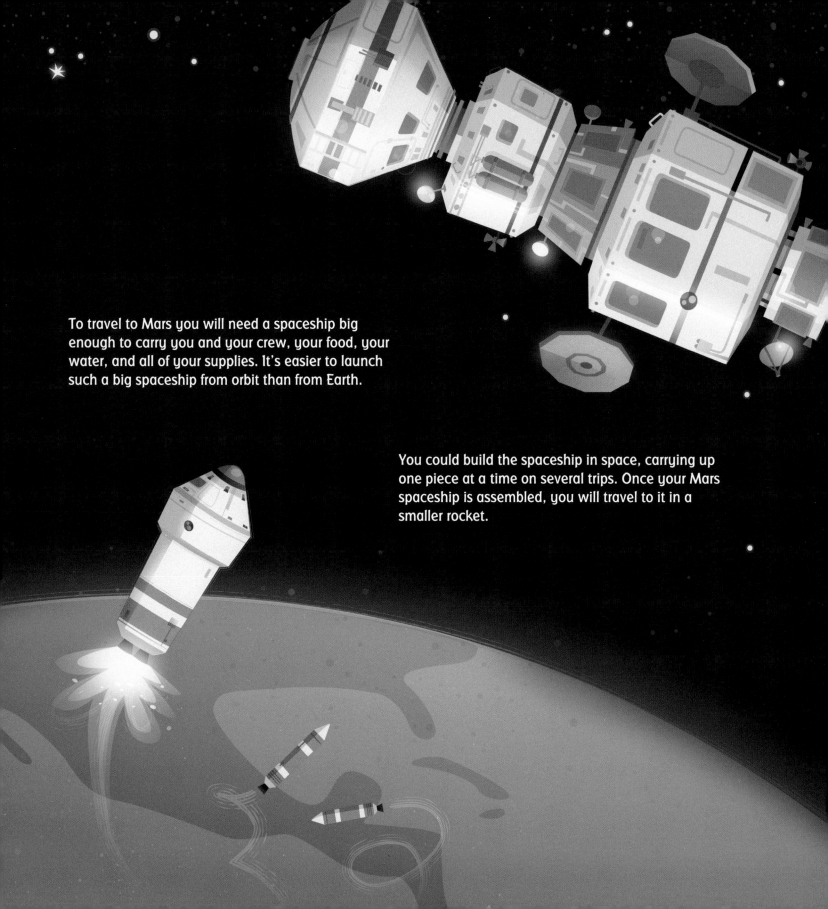

To travel to Mars you will need a spaceship big enough to carry you and your crew, your food, your water, and all of your supplies. It's easier to launch such a big spaceship from orbit than from Earth.

You could build the spaceship in space, carrying up one piece at a time on several trips. Once your Mars spaceship is assembled, you will travel to it in a smaller rocket.

There is no air to breathe in space. When your rocket reaches the spaceship, the two spacecraft will be locked together. Then the doors—or hatches—will open to let you out of your rocket and into the spaceship. That will keep air inside the spacecraft.

Let's dive through the hatch,
Let's dive through the hatch,
Hey-ho, to Mars we'll go—
Let's dive through the hatch.

Using current rocket engines, a trip to Mars would take about six months. But engineers are trying to develop new propulsion systems that might cut that time in half. They are also exploring ways to mimic gravity in a spacecraft. With present-day technology, you would not feel the effect of gravity so far from a planet's surface. You would float!

Imagine what a mess you could make without gravity. At home, if you leave your toys on the floor, they stay where you dropped them. But in space, anything you don't put in a cupboard or fasten in place will drift like dandelion fluff, bouncing off walls and your crewmates.

Can you catch my sock?
Can you catch my sock?
Hey-ho, to Mars we'll go—
Can you catch my sock?

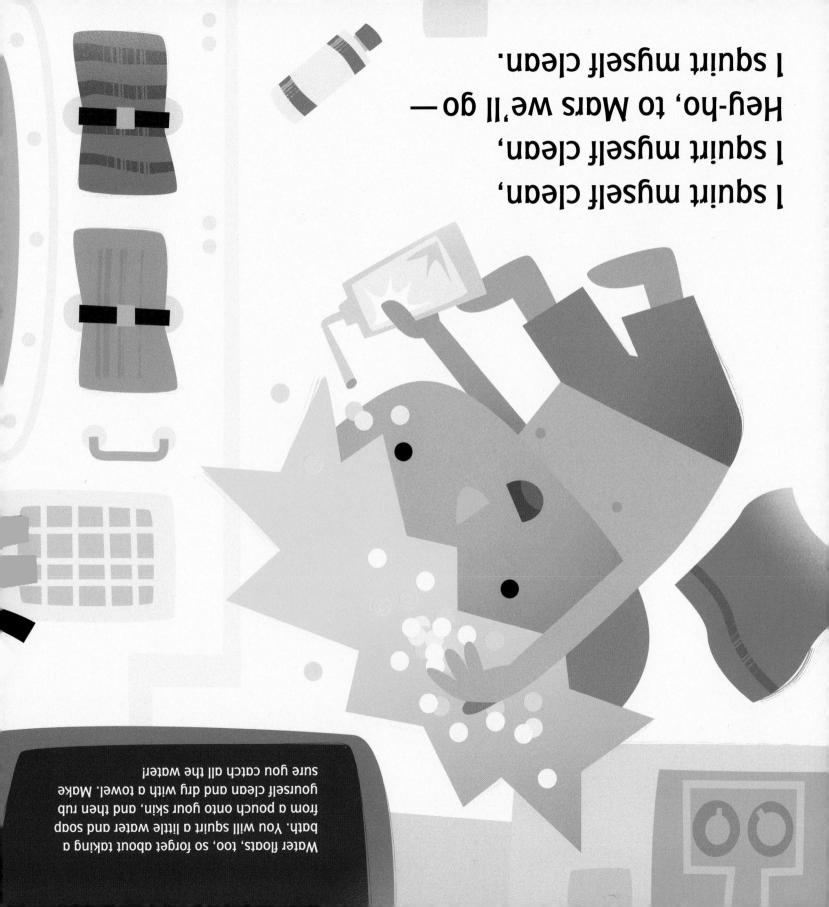

I squirt myself clean,
I squirt myself clean,
Hey-ho, to Mars we'll go —
I squirt myself clean.

Water floats, too, so forget about taking a bath. You will squirt a little water and soap from a pouch onto your skin, and then rub yourself clean and dry with a towel. Make sure you catch all the water!

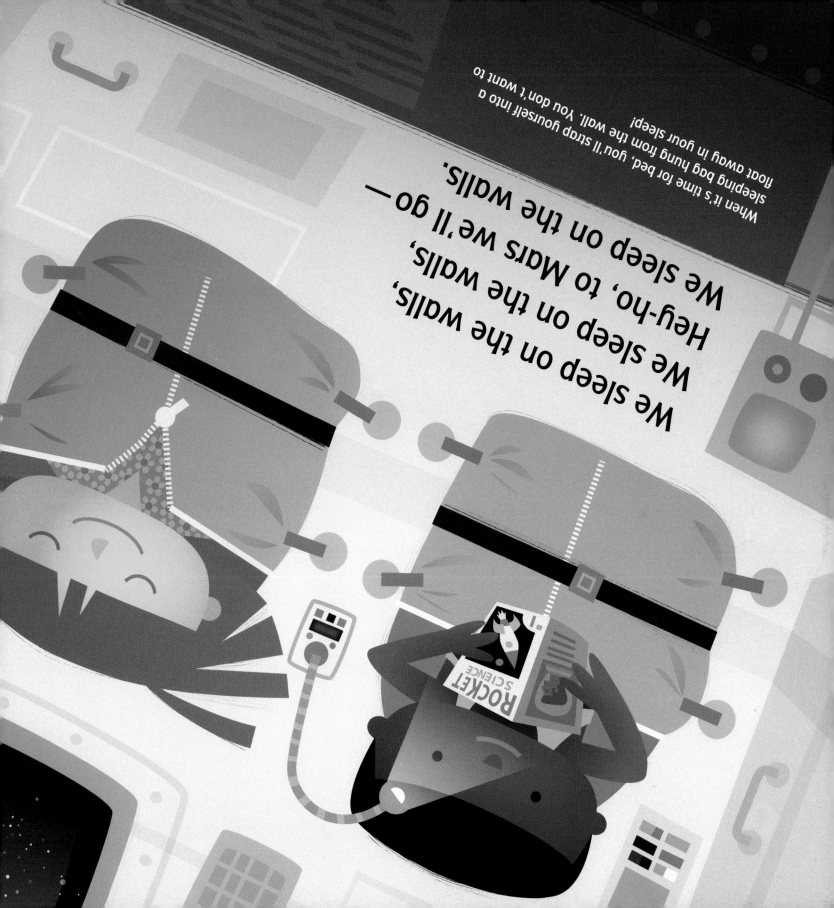

We sleep on the walls,
We sleep on the walls,
Hey-ho, to Mars we'll go,
We sleep on the walls.

When it's time for bed, you'll strap yourself into a sleeping bag hung from the wall. You don't want to float away in your sleep!

ROCKET SCIENCE

Our greens grow in bags,
Our greens grow in bags,
Hey-ho, to Mars we'll go —
Our greens grow in bags.

For a trip to Mars, you will need to bring enough food to last you at least two years. Most of the food will be packaged on Earth, but you can also grow fresh vegetables in bags or other containers that hold nutrients and moisture—no dirt needed. Add special lamps that mimic sunlight, and you're a space farmer.

On Earth, lifting your feet when you walk or run helps make your bones and muscles strong. In space, without gravity constantly pulling on you, those bones and muscles grow weak. To keep fit, you will need to exercise every day.

How long till we're there?
How long till we're there?
Hey-ho, to Mars we'll go—
How long till we're there?

On your journey to Mars, you won't be able to go outside to play. But you can do many of the things you might do on a rainy day at home: watch movies, read, play games, or daydream about the adventures to come.

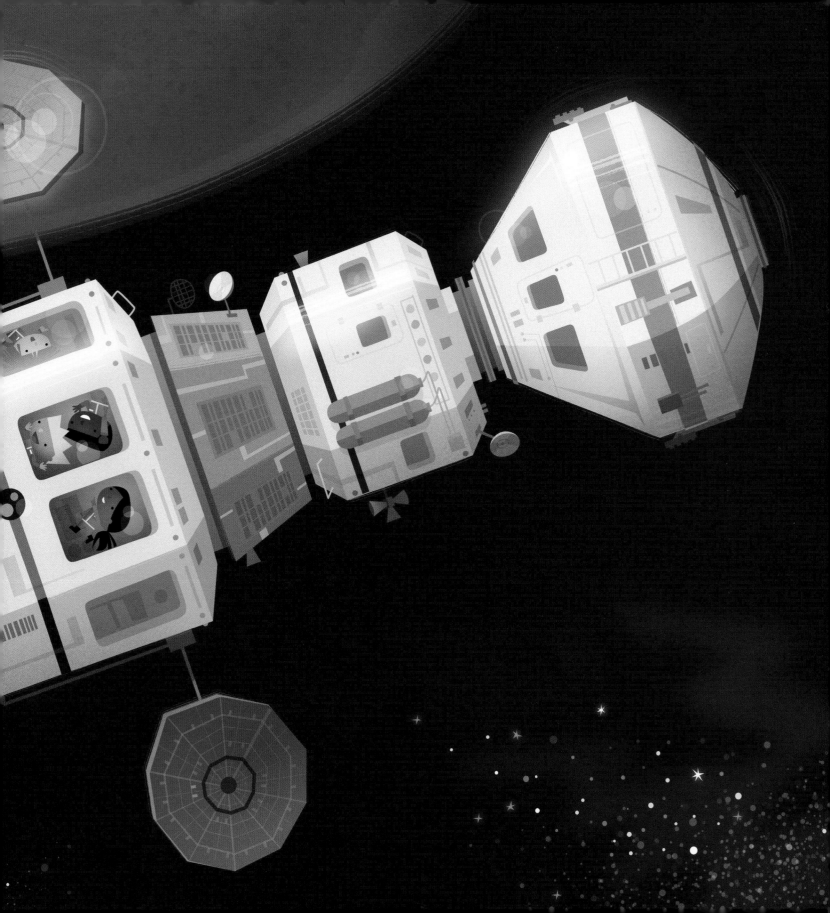

After your long space voyage, you will arrive at Mars. Although the gravity of Mars is weaker than that of Earth, you will not land your big spacecraft there. Instead, you will leave your spacecraft in orbit and travel to the surface in a lander.

Touchdown! We've arrived.
Touchdown! We've arrived.
Hey-ho, to Mars we'll go—
Touchdown! We've arrived.

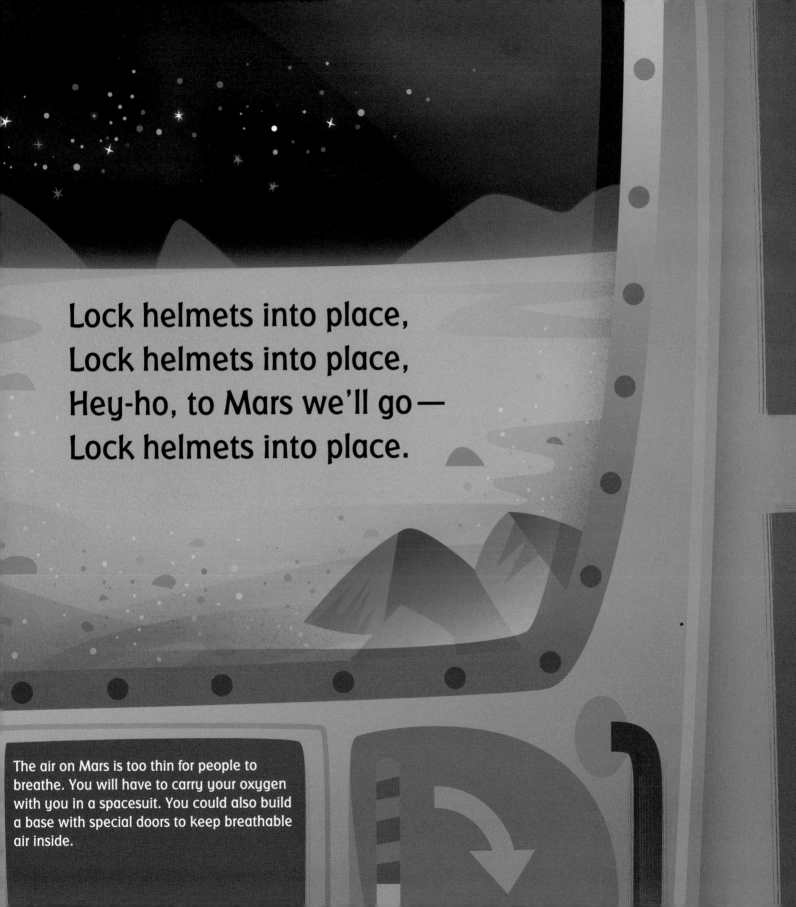

Lock helmets into place,
Lock helmets into place,
Hey-ho, to Mars we'll go —
Lock helmets into place.

The air on Mars is too thin for people to breathe. You will have to carry your oxygen with you in a spacesuit. You could also build a base with special doors to keep breathable air inside.

Have you ever looked at Mars in the night sky? It's a reddish point of light, no brighter than most of the stars. When you're millions of miles away on Mars, Earth will look like a small blue dot in the Martian sky.

The Earth's a blue dot,
The Earth's a blue dot,
Hey-ho, to Mars we'll go—
The Earth's a blue dot.

Come on, let's explore,
Come on, let's explore,
Hey-ho, to Mars we'll go—
Come on, let's EXPLORE!

With a whole planet to explore, what will you see first? Valles Marineris, a canyon five times deeper than the Grand Canyon? Olympus Mons, a volcano nearly three times higher than the tallest mountain on Earth? Astronauts visiting Mars may stay as long as two years, so you will have plenty of time to explore.

Sending astronauts to the Moon was hard; sending people to Mars will be much harder. Between Earth and Mars lie millions of miles of space. The orbits of the two planets move them closer and farther apart during two-year cycles. The distance between them is never less than 33 million miles and is usually far greater, up to 249 million miles. It took astronauts three days to travel to the Moon, but journeys to Mars could take six months each way.

The United States, Russia, Europe, Japan, and India have all sent unmanned, robotic spacecraft to Mars. Some missions have succeeded in landing rovers to explore the Martian surface. Other spacecraft have orbited the planet, sending back information that will one day help us plan human missions to Mars.

Before astronauts make the trip, scientists will need to develop the following:

- A spacecraft that can carry humans to Mars and back on a two-year mission

- Reliable methods to grow food in space

- Equipment on Mars to create breathable air

- A way to manufacture rocket fuel on Mars for the return trip—or a propulsion method that does not need large amounts of fuel

- An environment that ensures the health of astronauts on a long mission

After Earth, Mars is the most habitable planet in our solar system. Learning more about our neighbor will teach us more about how planets develop, how atmospheres form and change, and how life may survive on different worlds. Of course, exploring Mars will also be a grand adventure. Do you want to go?

Learn more about Mars exploration:

Robotic Mars Exploration (NASA): http://www.nasa.gov/mars

Mars for Kids (NASA): http://mars.nasa.gov/participate/funzone/

Mars—the Red Planet (European Space Agency):
https://www.esa.int/esaKIDSen/SEM3L6WJD1E_OurUniverse_0.html

Note: Distances and sizes of objects in art are not to scale.

To Lu Coffing, who's definitely not a mundane—S. L.

For my exploring-the-world adventure friends, Mark, Jen, and Lisa—B. K.

Special thanks to David F. Doody, robotic-spaceflight engineer, author of *Deep Space Craft: An Overview of Interplanetary Flight*, and publisher of Blüroof Press, for reviewing the text and art for accuracy.

First paperback edition 2019
Text copyright © 2018 by Susan Lendroth
Illustrations copyright © 2018 by Bob Kolar

Published by Charlesbridge, 85 Main Street, Watertown, MA 02472
(617) 926-0329 · www.charlesbridge.com

Library of Congress Cataloging-in-Publication Data
Names: Lendroth, Susan, author.
Title: Hey-ho, to Mars we'll go!: a space-age version of the Farmer in the dell / Susan Lendroth.
Other titles: Hey-ho, to Mars we will go
Description: Watertown, MA: Charlesbridge, [2018]
Identifiers: LCCN 2016053959 (print) | LCCN 2016059786 (ebook) |
ISBN 9781580897440 (reinforced for library use) | ISBN 9781623541002 (softcover)
| ISBN 9781632895615 (ebook) | ISBN 9781632895622 (ebook pdf)
Subjects: LCSH: Mars (Planet)—Juvenile literature. | Mars (Planet)—Exploration—Juvenile literature.
Classification: LCC QB641 .L421 2018 (print) | LCC QB641 (ebook) | DDC 629.45/53—dc23
LC record available at https://lccn.loc.gov/2016053959

Printed in China
(hc) 10 9 8 7 6 5 4 3 2 1
(sc) 10 9 8 7 6 5 4 3 2 1

Artwork was created with a computer, which kind of makes Bob Kolar an artist and a scientist.
Display type set in Swung Note by Pintassilgo Prints and hand-lettered by Bob Kolar
Text type set in Badger by Red Rooster Collection
Color separations by Colourscan Print Co Pte Ltd. in Singapore
Printed by 1010 Printing Company International Limited in Huizhou, Guangdong, China
Production supervision by Brian G. Walker
Designed by Susan Mallory Sherman